WE
THE PEOPLE
JOHN PAUL JONES

Published by Creative Education, Inc. 123 South
Broad Street, Mankato, Minnesota 56001

Library of Congress Cataloging-in-Publication Data

Zadra, Dan.
    John Paul Jones : naval hero, 1747-1792 / Dan Zadra ; illustrated
by John Keely.

    p. cm. — (We the people)
    Summary: A brief biography of John Paul Jones, stressing his naval
career and activities during the Revolutionary War.
    ISBN 0-88682-193-2
    1. Jones, John Paul, 1747-1792—Juvenile literature.   2. Admirals—
United States—Biography—Juvenile literature.   3. United States.
Navy—Biography—Juvenile literature.   4. United States—History—
Revolution, 1775-1783—Naval operations—Juvenile literature.
[1. Jones, John Paul, 1747-1792.   2. United States—History—
Revolution, 1775-1783—Biography.]   I. Keely, John, ill.
II. Title.   III. Series.
E207.J7Z33   1988
973.3'5'0924—dc19
[B]   87-36388
[92]   CIP
                                                                  AC

WE
THE PEOPLE
JOHN PAUL JONES

NAVAL HERO
(1747-1792)

DAN ZADRA

Illustrated By John Keely

CREATIVE EDUCATION

JOHN PAUL JONES

It wasn't easy to say good-bye to his parents. After all, he was only 13 years old. But young John Paul, Jr., had made up his mind to become a "sailor man."

In 1761, he left his home in Arbigland, Scotland and set sail to Fredericksburg, Virginia, as a cabin boy to a merchant. At first, the rough, dark ocean frightened him and made him seasick. But John Paul was still excited and happy. He knew that he had made the right decision. His great adventure had begun.

At Fredericksburg, John visited his older brother, William, who had also left Scotland to live in America. After living with William for a while, John yearned for the open sea and enlisted as an apprentice on a swift, two-masted brigantine. For three years, he sailed between Scotland, the West Indies, and Virginia in the American colonies.

Then John wanted to learn the

duties of a ship's officer. Though still
a teen-ager, he became chief mate on
a slave ship in 1766. It was a horrible
experience. Many slaves died from
sickness, or drowned while trying to
escape. "This is wrong," thought

John. "No one should be a slave."

In 1768, he quit his job on the slaver and sailed home to Scotland as a passenger. While at sea, the ship's captain and mate died of a fever. It was up to John Paul to get the vessel safely to port. He did this so well that the ship's owners made him a captain at the age of 21. The beautiful and dangerous West Indies would be his route.

Swiftly, Captain John Paul earned a reputation as one of the best—and toughest—skippers on the open seas. His youth and his short stature (five feet, six inches) put him at a disadvantage when dealing with salty old sailors. So he bolstered his confidence by wearing elegant clothes and carrying a sword. If a sailor was slow to obey, Captain Paul had him flogged.

One man who was whipped later took sick of a fever and died. Charges were brought against John Paul. When the courts cleared him completely, John became even a worse tyrant to his men.

Captain Paul's hot temper finally ruined his civilian career. In 1773, his ship anchored at the West Indies island of Tobago. The crew wanted money, but John refused to give it to them. One ringleader from among the crew tried to strike the captain with a club.

Overcome with fury, John killed the man with his sword. Rather than wait in prison for trial, John escaped from Tobago and fled to Virginia.

From then on, the English branded him a fugitive. To hide his identity, John Paul changed his name to John Paul "Jones."

A year later, in 1775, the outbreak of the Revolutionary War brought John Paul Jones out of hiding. He set off to Philadelphia where he enlisted in the brand-new Continental Navy as a lieutenant.

In Spring, 1776, the entire American Navy consisted of eleven vessels of various sizes. Eight of them went off to raid the Bahama Islands. Senior Lieutenant Jones served on the flagship, *Alfred.* Later that year he was promoted to Captain of the small, swift sloop, *Providence.*

Now, the hot-tempered Jones sailed boldly after the larger British

warships. In daring raids, he swiftly captured seven vessels as prizes-of-war and crippled several others.

Jones became an overnight hero.

He was given command of the *Alfred*. Sailing up toward Canada, he captured more prizes and sent several British frigates on the run.

When he returned to port, he expected to be promoted. Unfortunately, he had made many enemies because of his bad temper and criticism of other officers. Even worse, he was not American-born. Congress still regarded him as a "foreigner." John Paul Jones was bitter and hurt, but he still returned to duty for America on his old ship, the *Providence*.

Then, in 1777, Jones was sent to France to take delivery of a new vessel. While in Paris, he became the friend of Benjamin Franklin, the famous statesman-scientist and author of *Poor Richard's Almanac*.

It was Franklin who helped persuade France to declare war on Britain. When this happened, in 1778, Jones was given permission to use French ports as a base for raiding

England. This was bad news indeed for the British Navy!

On his first of many daring missions in English waters, Jones took the warship *Ranger* and attacked the British town of Whitehaven not far from his own birthplace. Then, in a spectacular battle, he captured an important British warship, *H.M.S. Drake.* Now, people in England

wrote songs about the daring Yankee raider.

The next year, Jones was given command of the *Duras*, a ship twice as big as the *Ranger*. He changed the name of his new vessel to *Bonhomme Richard* (Goodfellow Richard), in honor of Ben Franklin's almanac.

With Captain Jones leading the way aboard the *Bonhomme Richard*, a fleet of five American vessels went raiding around Ireland and Scotland, capturing many prize ships and infuriating the British King.

Then, on September 23, 1779, Captain Jones spotted a convoy of 41 British merchant ships, guarded by two of Britain's mightiest men-of-war.

With her rows of cannon loaded and ready, the British frigate *H.M.S. Serapis* caught the wind and slashed swiftly toward the *Richard*. John Paul Jones was in a desperate position. Compared to the *Serapis*, his ship was too slow and out-gunned. He knew at once that his only chance lay in charging *Serapis* and boarding her.

Cannons blazing, the two ships drifted together. The noble *Richard*

took a fearful pounding and many guns were knocked out of action. But Jones stood firmly on the deck of his ship, with his sword and pistol at the ready, urging his men to keep their courage.

At the last moment, the British captain tried to sail around the *Richard.* But Jones's ship rammed the Britisher's stern.

The English captain confidently called out, asking if Jones was ready to surrender.

John Paul Jones shouted back: "I have not yet begun to fight!"

For two more hours the ships clung together, tied by grappling cables. *Richard* began to sink. Surely, Captain Jones would have to surrender soon.

But French musketeers aboard the *Richard* kept on sniping at British gunners. Then a miracle! Somehow, a brave Yankee sailor crawled out on a mast and dropped grenades into the hold of *Serapis*, exploding her powder. Then Jones, with only three cannons left, managed to topple the mainmast of *Serapis*. That did the trick. The British ship surrendered. Jones sailed the captured *Serapis* back to France. The gallant *Bonhomme Richard* sank two days after the great battle, but history has kept her noble deeds afloat.

In 1780, Ben Franklin asked John Paul Jones to sail to America with a cargo of badly-needed supplies. At the time, the French nobility were making a great fuss over the heroic captain, inviting him to their fancy dress balls. Captain Jones was very reluctant to leave Paris. But duty called, so he set sail.

Back in Philadelphia, Jones was at first hailed as a hero. But then his old habit of criticizing others made him seem a nuisance and a bore.

Congress refused to make him an admiral. When the war ended, the Navy was abolished. Jones protested in vain that America still needed its Navy in order to survive as a nation. He begged Congress to rebuild the Navy and set up an academy to train officers. But no one listened—then.

In 1787, John Paul Jones left America and went to live in Paris, where he felt people were friendly to his ideas. As a captain without a ship, however, he did not know what to do with himself. Finally, Empress Catherine of Russia offered him the post of Rear Admiral, and for one year he commanded a squadron of ships in the Black Sea. He took a leading role in helping the Russians defeat the Turks in the Second Battle of Liman. But jealous Russian captains made sure that Jones received little credit for his bravery.

Bitter and frustrated, Jones resigned from the Russian Navy in 1790 and went back to Paris. In 1792, he was appointed U.S. envoy to Al-

giers, an honor that would have pleased him. Sadly, however, John Paul Jones died of pneumonia before the commission arrived.

He was buried in the St. Louis Cemetery in Paris. But Americans finally came to understand and appreciate the deeds and beliefs of John Paul Jones. President Theodore Roosevelt sent vessels of the U.S. Navy to France in 1905, to bring his body back home. The great naval hero of the American Revolution was finally laid to rest in a place of honor in the chapel of the U.S. Naval Academy at Annapolis in 1913.

WE THE PEOPLE SERIES

WOMEN OF AMERICA

CLARA BARTON
JANE ADDAMS
ELIZABETH BLACKWELL
HARRIET TUBMAN
SUSAN B. ANTHONY
DOLLEY MADISON

INDIANS OF AMERICA

GERONIMO
CRAZY HORSE
CHIEF JOSEPH
PONTIAC
SQUANTO
OSCEOLA

FRONTIERSMEN OF AMERICA

DANIEL BOONE
BUFFALO BILL
JIM BRIDGER
FRANCIS MARION
DAVY CROCKETT
KIT CARSON

WAR HEROES OF AMERICA

JOHN PAUL JONES
PAUL REVERE
ROBERT E. LEE
ULYSSES S. GRANT
SAM HOUSTON
LAFAYETTE

EXPLORERS OF AMERICA

COLUMBUS
LEIF ERICSON
DeSOTO
LEWIS AND CLARK
CHAMPLAIN
CORONADO